Cancún

The Cubby
2024 Long Weekend Guide

James Cubby

**NO BUSINESS HAS PAID A SINGLE PENNY OR GIVEN _ANYTHING_
TO BE INCLUDED IN THIS BOOK.**

**The Cubby
Long Weekend Guide**

TABLE OF CONTENTS

**Chapter 1
FIRST THINGS FIRST – 4**
Why Cancún?
Transportation & Tips for Getting Around
Information

**Chapter 2
LODGING – 11**
Budget – Mid-Range - Luxury

**Chapter 3
RESTAURANTS – 30**
Budget – Mid-Range - Pricey

**Chapter 4
NIGHTLIFE – 45**

**Chapter 5
ATTRACTIONS – 53**
Water Sports

**Chapter 6
SHOPPING & SERVICES – 65**

INDEX – 68

Chapter 1
FIRST THINGS FIRST

Why Cancún?

Being world travelers, we knew the reputation of Cancún. We knew that Cancún is the Mecca of spring breakers and pasty Americans desperately seeking a weekend respite from biting winters. So it was with trepidation that, years ago, we first stepped foot on that hotel-covered sandbar. We dutifully wiggled into our bathing suits, slathered ourselves in sunblock, and walked out onto the beach. And then we finally understood it – we got why millions of people every year flock to this far corner of the

Yucatán Peninsula. *Cancún has got a world-class beach.*

We have been on many beaches around the world. And none of them are quite as magical as the one in Cancún. The sun is strong, but a constant gentle breeze keeps one comfortable. On first sight, you will not believe the color of the water you're looking at actually exists in nature. It really is a clear, bright turquoise. Waves lap gently on fine sand the color of cappuccino. The slope is very gradual, so you can head far into the water and still touch the bottom. And the temperature of the water is perfect year-round.

But there is more. There is something else about this beach that we just can't put our finger on. There is an idyllic serenity the likes of which we have never encountered before or since. Here we find an eclectic mix of all kinds, local and tourist. Here we find an elderly couple holding hands staring at the sea, a few yards from a group of beer-chugging frat boys. And all the people have a blissed-out, faraway smile on their faces. Yes, there is something magical about the beach in Cancún.

Mind you, Cancún is a tourist town. By far, the local industry is tourism, and most of what goes on in Cancún is designed to separate you from what you have in your wallet. If you are looking to get to know the culture and people the Yucatán Peninsula, Cancún is not the place for you. It is for good reason that Yucatecans call Cancún "Gringolandia." If you want to experience the true culture of the area, you will have to go to the ancient city of nearby Mérida.

Transportation & Tips for Getting Around

AIRPORT & TAXIS

Cancún Airport can be an unnerving and high-pressure experience. As soon as you disembark, you'll encounter dozens of pushy vendors representing various businesses, all trying to sell you (and sell you *hard*) a timeshare or a tour, or even just a taxi ride. The taxi people and cabbies can be very pushy. Take my advice and do yourself a favor—book yourself a pickup service before you arrive. They will meet you as you arrive and usher you through the craziness to your waiting van. You'll be at your hotel before you know it. (Many hotels offer free transfers—check to be sure.)

Rates from the airport run up to $60 one way, 20-mile trip to the Zona Hotelera (Hotel Zone). They only charge you half when you go the other way.

SHUTTLE SERVICE

A cheaper shuttle service is operated by Hertz and the Green Line. It runs every half hour. Buy your ticket when you get here.

BUS SERVICE

There's bus service from the airport into Cancun that runs just a few dollars.

RENTING A CAR

Renting a car is a great way to explore the many opportunities the Yucatán Peninsula has to offer. I recommend reserving your car ahead of time. When renting your car, it is ***very important*** that you specifically request insurance equal to the value of the car. It is not made clear when you pick it up, but you are personally responsible for any damage to the car. Upon return you are at the mercy of the staff for any scratch, so be very aware of the condition of the vehicle when you get it and make sure each ding and dent is noted in the rental agreement before you drive away. It's better to arrange your rental before you leave on your trip to be assured you get a car. All the major car rental firms are represented here.

CANCUN MUNICIPAL TOURISM OFFICE
Corner of Avenida Nader & Avenida Cobá: 998-887-3379. Open weekdays.

CANCUN CONVENTION BUREAU
www.cancun.travel (no .com after travel)

GENERAL INFORMATION
www.cancun.com
www.cancuntips.com

HOTEL

Chapter 2
LODGINGS

Timeshares

Budget - Cuidad Cancun (Downtown)

Budget - Isla Cancun (Beach-Zona Hotelera)
Moderate – Isla Cancun (Beach-Zona Hotelera)
Luxury – Isla Cancun (Beach-Zona Hotelera)

TIMESHARES

A word about timeshares. Many hotels and resorts in Cancún are associated with timeshare programs. Visitors are often invited to a timeshare presentation in return for a complimentary gift, such as a free meal. We urge you to attend the presentation ONLY IF YOU ARE SINCERELY INTERESTED IN A TIMESHARE. We have been to more timeshare presentations than we care to think about and we can assure you the complimentary gift is never worth the inconvenience. Sales techniques are tricky and often high-pressure, and more than one innocent vacationer has awakened the next day with a bad case of buyer's remorse. So if you are approached with a timeshare invitation, we urge you to firmly say NO and walk away. These people (they're under a lot of pressure themselves because they only get paid after they fleece you) do not give a damn about you, and you can't—*repeat, CAN'T*—hurt their feelings. So do not give them the time of day.

XBALAMQUÉ
Av. Yaxchilán 31, Sm. 22, Mz. 17, Quintana Roo,
Cancun: +52 998 892 3377
www.xbalamque.com
This place is a real find. The furnishings are very
much reflective of the countryside, with great tile-
work. They've tried to make the whole place look
very Mayan, with yard after yard of murals, paintings
and sculptures done in that style. All the furniture is
very rough-hewn (but you'll wish you had a few
pieces when you get back home.) There's a
refreshingly calming waterfall in the pool area.
There's a beautifully quaint courtyard and they have a

few junior suites. (Food in the Adelita restaurant is good, too, and those cool local beers are great.)

Budget - Isla Cancun (Beach-Zona Hotelera)

GRAND ROYAL LAGOON
Calle Quetzal No. 8-A | Boulevard Kukulcán Km 7.5, 52-998-883-2749/866-238-4218
https://bighotels.org/product/grand-royal-lagoon/
If you want to stay in the Hotel Zone on a budget, then this is the place for you. It is interestingly located on the back side of the sandbar on the lagoon, so don't expect to walk out your door onto the beach. But the beach is in walking distance, and all beachfront is common property in Mexico, so feel free to use another hotel's beach. It is also a short walk to shopping and the big clubs the zone is known for. The rooms are basic and clean; the showers are big with plenty of hot water and good pressure. Most rooms have kitchenettes. We recommend upgrading to a balcony for $10. The breakfast is tasty.

HOTEL DEL SOL
Av. Lopez Portillo Mz 2Lt 1A SM85, Puerto Juarez, Mexico: 52-998-880-3693/ +1-888-611-0574
www.hotel-del-sol.cancunhotelmexico.net/en
This hotel is not in Cancún proper, it is in Puerto Juarez, about eight kilometers north of Cancún, so it is a bit far from the all the attractions of the city and the Hotel/Beach Zone. It is, however, perfectly located forsea ad excursions to Isla de Mujeres, with

the ferry right across the street. The hotel has excellent views of the ocean, but there is no serviceable beach for miles, and there is no pool. The rooms are very clean and the service efficient.

HOTEL EL REY DEL CARIBE
Av. Uxmal 24 | Corner of Uxmal and Nader, Cancún 77500, Mexico:
52-998-884-2028
www.reycaribe.com
This lovely hotel can be appropriately described as an oasis. It is located in downtown Cancún, but once you've entered the compound you feel as though you've entered another world. The gardens are simply wonderful. You'll enjoy the hammocks by the pool. This is an eco-conscious hotel, so you'll appreciate all the green touches. The rooms are big, and on the upper floors include a kitchenette.

TERRACARIBE HOTEL
Av Lopez Portillo 70 | Esquina Av. Bonampak, Cancún 77500, Mexico:
52 998 211 3015, 1-800-837-7222

https://terracaribehotelboutique.com-cancun.com/
This place likes to bill itself as a boutique hotel. It's
not a boutique hotel, it's just a plain no-frills hotel.
But it is a clean hotel with good service. The staff
here are very friendly. The downside is the location,
it is in the city and the neighborhood is a little rustic.
The restaurant food is tasty, and the bar offers good
drinks and great service. All in all, a great value.

SOTAVENTO HOTEL AND YACHT CLUB
Blv. Kukulkan km 4 Zona Hotelera | Lote D.8.3 Calle
Pescador, Cancún 77500, Mexico: +52 998 127 5063
http://www.hotelsotavento.info/
Located on the northern edge of the Beach/Hotel
Zone across the street from the beach hotels and
overlooking the lagoon. It is a basic no-frills hotel
with a nice pool and garden area.

SUITES GABY HOTEL
Av. Sunyaxche Lote 46 y 47 | Mza 2 Supermanzana
25 CP, Cancún 77509, Mexico: 52-998-887-8037
https://www.suitesgaby.com.mx/index
A decent basic hotel in the center of Cancún. The
rooms are clean with internet available. It is
conveniently located near the bus station and also
quite close to the tourist market.

ALL RITMO RESORT & WATERPARK

Km 1.5 Carretera a Punta Juarez-Punta
Sam, Cancún 77500, Mexico: +52 998 478 5052
/ 877-734-3186
www.allritmocancun.com
 As you can tell from the name, this is a very kid-
friendly resort. But it is also lots of fun for adults.
The staff is very keyed in to entertaining and offering
a good time. There are all sorts of activities offered,
such as the waterpark, games, snorkeling, boating and
surprisingly good Vegas-style shows in the evening.
The rooms are very large and well maintained. The
hotel is located off the tourist strip, up north a bit in
Puerto Juarez, and is conveniently located near the
ferry to Isla Mujeres.

AVALON BACCARA

Blvd. Kukulcan Km 11.5 | Zona
Hotelera, Cancún 77500, Mexico:
998-881-3900/ 1-800-507-1239

www.hotelavalonbaccaracancun.com
The Avalon Baccara, is, put simply, an excellent hotel. It is quiet and intimate. There are only about 30 rooms in the hotel. The setting is peaceful and out of the way. The staff, from the management to the maids, is consistent in the superior service they offer. The rooms are spotless and relaxing, each one featuring a balcony with Jacuzzi. The grounds are well-kept, from the colorful pool to the groomed beach. The food is delicious. We can't recommend enough the Avalon Baccara.

KRYSTAL GRAND PUNTA CANCUN

Blvd Kukulcan Km 9, Hotel Zone, Cancún 77500, Mexico:
+ 52 998-848-9800
www.krystal-cancun.com/?card=1
The building is a bit dated but is well-maintained. The lobby tends to get a bit warm, but the rooms have excellent AC. The hotel is tall, so the upper floors have excellent views no matter what side you are one. Location is everything, and the Krystal has excellent location. The hotel sits in a quiet cul-de-sac just next to the nightclub zone and restaurants. It also boasts one of the best sections of beach, where the water is most calm.

LE BLANC SPA

Blvd. Kukulkan Km. 10, Cancún, 888-702-0913
https://cancun.leblancsparesorts.com/
An adults-only beach all-inclusive resort offers 260 rooms with balconies featuring great ocean or lagoon views – many with sitting areas and whirlpool tubs.

Amenities include flat-screen LED TVs, Bvlgari bath amenities, 24-hour butler services, complimentary Wi-Fi, complimentary breakfast and parking. Hotel facilities include: 4 on-site dining options, 6 bars, fitness center, golf course, outdoor pools, and the **Blanc Spa** (with those long white curtains billowing in the breeze, just like in the movies). Beach access. AAA Five Diamond Award.

MARRIOTT CASAMAGNA CANCÚN RESORT

Blvd Kukulcan, Retorno Chac L-41 | Zona Hotelera, Cancún 77500, Mexico: 52-998-881-2000
www.marriott.com
The Marriott offers everything you would expect from a resort hotel. Room service is quick. The rooms are large and clean. We recommend you spring for an ocean view. Also, when booking your room, get the package that includes the breakfast buffet. Trust us, you'll be glad you did. The CasaMagna breakfast buffet is the stuff of legends.

NIZUC RESORT & SPA

Blvd Kukulkan Mz 59 Lote 1-01 Km 21.26, Cancun, +52 998 891 5700
www.nizuc.com
An ideal resort for golf lovers, beachfront resort is located right next to a golf course. Though this is a large resort (about 30 acres), it feels much more intimate because of the mangroves surrounding the place. There's a barrier reef not far from the shore, so explore that when you go snorkeling. This resort offers 274 soundproofed rooms with high ceilings. The garden villas offer more privacy if that's what

you're looking for. The penthouse suites have "outdoor living rooms." Amenities include complimentary Wi-Fi, iPod docks, flat-screen TVs, Nespresso machines and minibars. Resort facilities include: 6 restaurants (including **Terra Nostra**, with an Italian motif and the modern Mexican spot **Ramona**), 2 lounge bars, 2 pools, tennis courts, a full-service spa, and a gym. Family friendly facility. Conveniently located near attractions like the Playa Delfines beach and the Interactive Aquarium.

WYNDHAM CANCÚN HOTEL
Blvd Kukulcan km 16.5, Hotel
Zone, Cancún 77500, Mexico: 52-998-881-0600
www.omnihotels.com
Still a good hotel, but it may be a bit on the old side. The beds are very comfortable, but the rooms are small and the bathrooms are smaller. You'll get great service from the staff, particularly the beach staff. The food is not very impressive, so head out when dining.

TEMPTATION RESORT SPA CANCÚN

Blvd. Kukulcan km 3.5 | Zona Hotelera/ Hotel
Zone, Cancún 77500, Mexico: 52-998-848-7900/
877-485-8367
https://www.temptation-experience.com/
Temptation is an all-inclusive adults-only resort,
which means you can eat and/or drink to your heart's
content, and you can probably find someone to do it
with you. There is a definite party atmosphere.
There are lots of ways to meet people, with activities
going on round the clock. It has a reputation as a bit
of a swingers' hotel. But you don't have to be a
horny single to enjoy the resort. There is a "sexy"
pool and there is a "quiet" pool. Rooms are clean,
staff is on the ball, and the food is pretty good. We
recommend The Wok restaurant.

WESTIN LAGUNAMAR CANCÚN

Km 12.5 Blvd Kukulcan | Zona Hotelera, PO Box
834 Apdo., Cancún 77500, Mexico: 52-998-891-4200
www.marriott.com/hotels
This is a timeshare resort. They are going to want
you to listen to their sales pitch, which we
recommend you avoid unless you really are
interested. The hotel facilities are top notch. All the
suites have wifi, balconies, washer/dryers, and
kitchens stocked with some basics. If cooking your
own food is not your idea of a vacation, the hotel is in
walking distance of some very excellent restaurants,
which the hotel staff will happily direct you to. They
will also help you with the myriad of activities
offered at the resort. The grounds are beautiful, and
their pool and fountain system is spectacular.

Luxury – Isla Cancun (Beach-Zona Hotelera)

EXCELLENCE RIVIERA

Carretera Federal 307 Chetumal, Puerto Juarez
| Manzana 7, Lote 1, S.M. 11, Puerto Morelos
77580, Mexico: 52-998-872-8500, 1-866-540-2585
www.excellence-resorts.com
The Excellence is an all-inclusive resort located in
Puerto Morelos, just south of Cancún. The staff
really stresses the notion that you are home. That is if
your home has hundreds of servants running around
anticipating your every wish. And should your wish
be a drink, then you are in the right spot. The bar
staff is very knowledgeable, and they serve only
quality brands. If you don't care for alcohol, we
highly recommend the cucumber lemonade.
Foodwise there are 8 on site restaurants to choose
from. Room service is quick and available 24 hours a
day.

FIESTA AMERICANA GRAND CORAL BEACH RESORT & SPA

Blvd Kukulcan Km 9.5 Lote 6 | Zona
Hotelera, Cancún 77500, Mexico:
+52 443 310 8137
www.grandfiestamericana.com
Just what you'd expect from a five-star hotel. The
staff is courteous and always there with anything you
need. The rooms are well-designed. Beds are
luxurious with lots of comfy pillows. The bathrooms
are almost entire suites in themselves. The food in
the restaurants is pricey, but well worth it. Despite

the name, this is not a party hotel – things quiet down after midnight, but it is within stumbling distance of the nightclubs.

RITZ-CARLTON

Retorno del Rey 36 | Zona Hotelera, Quintana Roo, Cancún 77500, Mexico: 52-998-881-0808 www.ritzcarlton.com

As one would expect from the Ritz-Carlton, this is a sumptuously laid out resort. The building and the grounds are beautiful. All that can be said of the rooms is they are perfect. The pool areas are luxurious and relaxing. The staff is always on the lookout for a way to make you more comfortable. The fitness area features state of the art equipment, and there is bottled water and fresh towels at every station. The beach, of course, is beautiful, relaxing and perfectly groomed. If you plan on using a cabana at the beach, reserve it ahead of time. Upgrading to the hotel's Club Level will get you ever more stellar services and luxury, and all food, drinks and alcohol are included. If you are a fan of the Ritz's exceptional food, which can be quite pricey, you can save considerably by upgrading.

RIU PALACE LAS AMERICAS

Blvd Kukulcan, Km 8.5, Manzana 50 | Lote 4, Zona
Hotelera, Cancún 77500, Mexico: 52-998-891-4300/
888-666-8816/ 1 888-325-8481
www.riu.com

All-inclusive resort on the Hotel-zone. The staff is
friendly. The building is a bit old, and by today's
standards, the rooms are small. Also, the walls are
rather thin, and you had better hope for a quiet
neighbor. That said, the staff is working constantly to
keep the grounds in good condition. The food is
pretty good, and there's lots of top-shelf booze. 24-
hour room service is also a nice touch.

LIVE AQUA ALL-INCLUSIVE

Boulevard Kukulcan Km. 12.5 Zona
Hotelera, Cancún 77500, Mexico: 52-998-881-7600/
800-343-7821
www.liveaqua.com/hoteles-y-resorts/live-aqua-beach-resort-cancun

The building here is very beautiful and well designed, there is a light and airy feel to the place. Walking into the lobby for the first time is an impressive sight. The pools are ubiquitous; you could swim in a different pool every day, and still not hit them all in a week. And in that week you will never see or hear a child… they are simply not allowed. The rooms are nice … great if you upgrade to a suite. The staff is friendly. Drinks can be a bit weak, so feel free to order an extra shot. We found the food at Live Aqua to be a bit weak also. Of the restaurant options, the best is MB.

MOON PALACE GOLF & SPA RESORT

Carretera Federal 307 Km
340, Cancún 77500, Mexico: 52-998-881-6000/ 800-986-5632
www.moonpalacecancun.com
All-inclusive. The resort is huge, so take advantage
of the many golf carts. All rooms have a balcony.
Obviously one of the big draws of this place are the
golf courses, which have been installed with a respect
for the local environment, so while you're teeing off,
you might get a chance to see a crocodile.

SUN PALACE

Blvd. Kukulcan KM. 20 | Zona
Hotelera, Cancún 77500, Mexico: 800-986-5632
www.palaceresorts.com
Devoted guests tend to come back to the Sun Palace
year after year. The staff is warm and friendly and
very accommodating. We recommend you upgrade
to the concierge level; the extra amenities and
superior room make it well worth it. All the rooms in
the hotel are large and comfortable. Our only issue is
the toilets in the bathrooms could stand to have some
privacy walls if you are going to be sharing the
bathroom.

THE ROYAL CANCÚN
Kukulkan Km 11.5 Hotel
Kukulcan Km. 4.5 Lotes C2 & C2A, Zona Hotelera,
77500 Cancún, QROO, Mexico, 954-368-1173/
Book: 1-888-387-4755
www.royalresorts.com
This is an excellent all-inclusive resort and the
flagship of Real Resorts. First class service through
and through. The rooms are fantastic. Finicky
sleepers will love the beds and appreciate the "Pillow
Menu." Each room has dispensers of call-brand
whiskey, vodka, rum and tequila. You are never at a
want for anything. There is a variety of different
restaurants in the hotel, most notable is the Asiana.
The hotel buffet is a little ho-hum. The beach is
always impeccably groomed. And for those of you
who can't stand to be out of touch, there is a strong
wifi signal everywhere.

Chapter 3
RESTAURANTS

Budget

100% NATURAL
Juices, Sandwiches, Lunch, Healthy, Vegetarian,
Vegan
Av. Sunyaxche lote 62, Supermanzana 25, Mza. 6
(Col. Centro), Cancún, Quintana Roo 77500, Mexico:
52-998-884-0102
No Website
100% Natural is a restaurant chain that is happily
taking Mexico by storm. The food offered is free of
preservatives and artificial flavors and colorings. For
breakfast, lunch and dinner, healthy fare is the theme.
The juice bar offers freshly made juices from local
fruits and veggies. The delicious whole-wheat bread

is baked fresh on-site, so try one of their tasty sandwiches. We recommend the veggie burger.

CALYPSO'S GRILL AND MEXICAN FOOD
Seafood, Mexican
Kukulcan Ave. km 8.5 next to Cancun
Center, Cancún 77500, Mexico:
52 998-883-1244 / 52 998-214-5393
No Website
Calypso's is a good basic no-frills restaurant in the Hotel Zone across from the Fiesta Americana. The owner, Felipe, is a character, and loves goofing around with his customers. The Mexican food is so-so. The Seafood is what we recommend. It's good eating, and a great value. The plate of Lobster Tails is our favorite item. And don't miss the house tequila.

RESTAURANTE LE NATURA
Mexican, Health, Vegetarian, Seafood
Boulevard Kukulcan km 9.5 | Zona
Hotelera, Cancún 77500, Mexico:
52 998-252-6799
www.restaurantenatura.com WEBSITE DOWN AT
PRESSTIME
Here is a great way to start your day in the Hotel
Zone. This inexpensive little eatery is right across the
street from Señor Frog's. They have a large variety
of fruit juices and smoothies they offer, including
some tasty options you've probably never had. Their
breakfast plates, such as the Juevos Rancheros, are

big and tasty. Or if you're into healthier fare you can get the fruit platter, which is huge. And you can get your breakfast served at any time of the day, which is a feature we always like. They don't stop at breakfast. There is a good selection of tasty dishes for both vegetarians and carnivores.

THE SURFIN BURRITO
Mexican
Kukulcan Blvd. Km 9.5, Cancún, Mexico: 52-998-883-0083
No Website
Absolutely the best burrito you will find in Cancún. It's just a little hut with some counters and stools, but it has great atmosphere. You make your selections on an order slip, and they build it for you… Hot and Huge. The tacos are good, but the burritos steal the

show. The smoothies are good too, and big. If you
prefer your drinks with a kick, they have a bar as
well. You might miss it, so remember it is right
across the street from Sr. Frog's next to the OXXO.
They are open 24 hours and they deliver to the hotel
zone.

LA TRANQUITA GRILL AND BAR
Pizza, Burgers, Steaks, Pastas
Ave. Kabah Mz1. Smz 13. Lote 22. Plaza Zona
Zentro, Cancún 77500, Mexico:
998-802-1841
www.latranquita.com
This little gem is located away from the tourist zone
in Cancún proper. It's a bit out of the way, so have
good directions or take a taxi. But once you've
gotten there you'll be glad you did. There is
something for everyone at La Tranquita, and it's all
good. It's better than good. Pizzas, burgers, steaks,
pastas, everything is delicious. The friendly staff
helmed by Manager Eric, who is always circulating
making sure his guests are enjoying their meal. The
space is warm and relaxing, and spotlessly clean.
Before you leave – and you won't want to leave –
have the corn cake for dessert.

Mid-Range

BACOLI TRATORIA
Blvd. Kulkukan, Km 17. Retorno Gucumatz,
52 998 283 3800
https://hotelesemporio.com
CUISINE: Italian
DRINKS: Full Bar
SERVING: Dinner
PRICE RANGE: $$
NEIGHBORHOOD: Quintana Roo
Located in Emporio Hotel & Resort, this eatery offers a creative menu of handmade Italian fare and pizzas prepared in a stone oven. Favorites: Calamari and Lasagna. Nice wine list.

ELEFANTA INDIAN CUISINE
Indian
Blvd. Kukulcan Km. 12.5 Zona Hotelera, Plaza La Isla, Cancún 77500, Mexico: 52-998-176-8070/ +52 998 144 0364
www.elefanta.com.mx
 Elefanta Indian is adjacent to Elefanta Thai, so whichever is your pleasure. The ambiance is superb; one feels transported to a bamboo paradise, overlooking an idyllic lagoon at sunset. The food is delicious. We love curry, and here it is made perfectly. Be advised that the pricing structure is such that you might feel nickel and dimed, and one is charged extra for such things as Rice and Naan.

FRED'S HOUSE & SEAFOOD

Seafood

Kukulkan Kilometro 14.5, Across from JW Marriott
Hotel, Cancún 77500, Mexico: 52-998-840-6467
https://fredshouserestaurant.com/

This is a seafood restaurant, so have the seafood. The
kitchen perfectly prepares and presents fish. We have
many favorites here. The house Seafood Platter
features a nice assortment of their best items. Start
with the Shrimp Ceviche. The Fresh Lobster, of
course, is a feast. And we also like the octopus,
which comes drenched in butter. We're very
impressed with the kid-friendly atmosphere here.
They even have an activity room for kids, complete
with video games. And while the kids are gone, have
one of Fred's Mojitos.

LOCANDA PAOLO

Italian, Seafood, Fusion

Bonampak Avenue 145 – Corner Jurel Street,
Cancún, Mexico: 52-998-887-2627
https://locandapaolo.com/

Eating at Locanda Paolo is a treat we highly
recommend to anyone. The whole event is a thrill for
the senses. The décor is modern and trendy, but not
cold. All customers are treated like VIPs by the
attentive staff, led by the owner, Paolo, who is very
hands-on. The menu is full of interesting and creative
dishes that delight the palate. We'd like to know
where they get their prosciutto because it is amazing.
And we're always happy to find a restaurant that
makes a good authentic Cream Puff!

MAKI TACO
Blvd. Kukulcan, 52 998 848 7500
https://oasishoteles.com/en/restaurants/maki-taco
CUISINE: Mexican/Japanese/Sushi
DRINKS: Full Bar
SERVING: Dinner, Closed Mon & Tues.
PRICE RANGE: $$$
NEIGHBORHOOD: Quintana Roo
Upscale hotel eatery offering a creative menu of a variety of cuisines. Excellent sushi. Favorites: Beef teriyaki and Cold calamari with mole sauce. Impressive tequila selection.

SAVIO'S BISTRO BY LA DOLCE
Italian
km 15 Zona Hotelera | Across from the Gran Meliá
Hotel, Cancún, Mexico:
52-998-884-3393
www.cancunitalianrestaurant.com
Located in the Hotel Zone, Savio's is the kind of
place you try once, and then you eat there several
times a week. The ambience is relaxed with dining
indoors and out. The staff is friendly and efficient.
All their food is consistently high quality and
delicious. We will name a few of our favorites:
Eggplant Parmesan, Veal Scallopini, Lasagna
Bollognaise, Calamari. The kitchen accommodates
special needs and requests.

Pricey

**CHIC CABARET & RESTAURANT COSTA
MUJERES**
Boulevard Vialidad Paseo Mujeres Sm 3 MZ 1 Lt 10,
52 998 868 5200
https://www.palladiumhotelgroup.com
CUISINE: Dinner Theater
DRINKS: Full Bar
SERVING: Dinner, Closed Mon & Tues.
PRICE RANGE: $$$$
NEIGHBORHOOD: Quintana Roo

Located in the palladium resort/TRS hotel, Chic Cabaret offers an energetic dinner show fusing dance, music and gastronomy, all in a dimly lit romantic room. The 7-course meal and drinks (which never stop coming) are all included in one price. Reservations recommended, as space is limited. Plan on a longish evening, starting at 7:30 or so and lasting till 11. With the dinner and the show, it stretches out.

HARRY'S PRIME STEAKHOUSE AND RAW BAR

Steak, Shellfish
Blvd. Kukulcan Km. 14.2,
No.1, Cancún 17520, Mexico: 52-998-840-6550
www.harrys.com.mx
Harry's is on par with any steakhouse you'll find in the US. They serve only imported Prime USDA or Kobe beef. The service is superb. The interior of the restaurant is simply stunning. The raw bar also offers an excellent selection of oysters. When you have had your fill, fill up a little more on dessert, of which our favorite is the Key Lime Pie. Their signature touch is a complimentary portion of Cotton Candy after the meal, which we find amusing.

L'ESCARGOT

French
Calle Pina #27, SM-25 | Quintana Roo
77500, Cancún, Mexico: 52-998-887-6337
http://lescargot.restaurantwebexperts.com/
Situated in a renovated house near downtown Cancún, a mother and daughter team have created a delicious haven for food lovers. The ambience is

cozy and warm, and the women give wonderful service. The food is delightful. There is an endless supply of delicious homemade bread. Our favorite dishes include the French Onion Soup and the Lamb. We also love their Patés.

LA PALAPA BELGA
European, International
Calle Quetzal No 13, Hotel Imperial
Laguna, Cancún 77500, Mexico:
52 998-883-5454
https://lapalapabelga.com.mx/
La Palapa Belga is the archetypal "hidden gem," located at the back of the Hotel Imperial Laguna. It can be a bit of a challenge to find, so we recommend taking a taxi. Once found, though you will be glad of the effort. The minimalist and rustic open-air restaurant is uniquely situated on the mainland side of lagoon, with a breathtaking view of the Hotel Zone across the water. The food here is consistently high

class. Only the best of restaurants can carry off a Duck Breast as well as here. We also recommend you indulge in the decadent Escargot. Our top pick for dessert… the Belgian Chocolate Mousse.

RESTAURANTE CAREYES
Blvd. Kukulcan Km. 16.5, +52 55 4170 9258
https://oasishoteles.com/en/restaurants/careyes
CUISINE: Seafood/Mexican/Steakhouse
DRINKS: Full Bar
SERVING: Lunch & Dinner, Closed Thursday
PRICE RANGE: $$$$
NEIGHBORHOOD: Quintana Roo
Elegant eatery serves traditional Mexican fare with a French twist. Favorites: Bacon Filet served with a side of oyster Rockefeller and Shrimp & Fish ceviche. Dress code.

RESTAURANTE CHIANTI
HOTEL NYX CANCUN
Blvd. Kukulkan Manzana 52 Km. 11.5, 52 998 848
9305
www.chiantirestaurant.net/dine-in.html
CUISINE: Italian
DRINKS: Full Bar
SERVING: Dinner, Closed Tuesdays
PRICE RANGE: $$$$
NEIGHBORHOOD: Quintana Roo
Upscale eatery offering a creative menu of authentic
Italian fare. Vegetarian options. Favorites: Pollo &
Gamberoni Alla Griglia (Large boneless breast of
chicken and large Gulf shrimp) and Ribeye Steak
topped with rich cream sauce with shallots and green
peppercorns. Excellent wine selection.

RESTAURANTE UMAMI
HOTEL NYX
Boulevard Kukulkan K.m. 11.5 Interior,
52 998 848 9311
www.nyxhotels.com
CUISINE: Japanese/Sushi
DRINKS: Full Bar
SERVING: Dinner
PRICE RANGE: $$$
NEIGHBORHOOD: Quintana Roo
Modern designed eatery offering incredible ocean
views. Great sushi. Favorites: Miso soup and
Sashimi. Creative cocktails.

SASI
Thai cuisine
CasaMagna Marriott Cancun Resort, Boulevard
Kukulcan, Retorno Chac L-41,
Cancún 77500, Mexico: +52 998-881 2092
www.sasi-thai.com
Sasi Thai is located on the grounds of the Casa
Magna Marriott. It has a wonderful ambience with
seating in thatched cubicles. The service is friendly
and efficient. They have the dishes you would expect
from a Thai restaurant, and we really enjoy the Pad
Thai. The Duck Curry is also quite tasty. We were
also quite charmed with the Chocolate Tamarind
Dessert.

TORA MEXICO
Blvd. Kukulcan Km. 15, 52 998 313 4128
https://torarestaurant.com.mx/
CUISINE: Japanese
DRINKS: Full Bar
SERVING: Lunch & Dinner
PRICE RANGE: $$$$
NEIGHBORHOOD: Quintana Roo
An upscale Japanese robata grill eatery offering
traditional Japanese cuisine with a modern influence.
Favorites: Ora King Salmon and Spicy Yellowtail
Sushi roll. Impressive cocktail selection.

THE WHITE BOX
GRAND OASIS PALM
Blvd. Kukulcan, 52 998 881 7000
https://oasishoteles.com/en/restaurants/the-white-box
CUISINE: Seafood/Steakhouse

DRINKS: Full Bar
SERVING: Dinner, Closed Mon & Tues.
PRICE RANGE: $$$$
NEIGHBORHOOD: Quintana Roo
Fine dining inspired by a group of renowned chefs.
Haute cuisine in small dishes. Great tasting menu.
Favorites: Blackened prawns and Sea Bass.
Impressive wine list. Only seats 20 so reservations
recommended.

Chapter 4
NIGHTLIFE

This is a party town. All those Spring Breakers didn't come down here to gaze lovesick at the moon. They came to party, to get drunk off tequila and to dance to loud music and to get laid.

Maybe you did, too!

In El Centro, prepare yourself for music that throbs incessantly, that's loud, that's insistent.

Like any good vacation destination, Cancun is just as fun at night as it is during the day. Most of the nightclubs are located in the entertainment district at the northeast tip of the Hotel Zone. Here you can party the night away in one mega-club, or bar hop to your heart's content.

The mega-bars have made Cancun famous for its nightlife. These monster party complexes hold thousands of people. They feature a variety of acts and eye-catching visuals as well as world-class DJs. The shows are constantly changing from moment to moment. At one moment you may be watching a contortionist, which might be followed by a bikini contest and fog machines. Internationally known performers regularly make appearances at these clubs. It is not uncommon to find such acts as Shakira or the Black-eyed Peas performing.

Coco Bongo is the oldest and most well-known of the mega-clubs, but others have come to prominence in recent years such as Bulldog, The City, Dady Rocks, and Dady O. Each of these places does its best to outdo the others, and we recommend visiting them on different nights. For those who haven't the time or stamina to visit one club a night there are nightclub tours that let you experience several of the mega-bars in one crazy night.

Drinks run $7 to $11.

It is not uncommon for the places to stay open until the sun comes up.

Here are some important tips for a safe and enjoyable night out in Cancun:

* Give your waiter a good tip up front, so they take care of you all night.

* Pay as you go, or you may be in for a big surprise.

* Keep your hands on your drink, and don't take a drink from a stranger. This goes for everybody, women and men alike.

   * If you've been drinking heavily, DO NOT go home alone or try to drive a car. One thing you don't want to deal with is the Mexican police and judicial systems, pathetically corrupt as they are. Also, DO NOT travel home alone. Have someone with you or take public transport. Don't even get into a cab alone if you can help it. You might end up in a ditch.
   * Don't leave your camera sitting around. Better yet, don't bring a camera at all.

THE CITY
Boulevard Kukulcán – KM 9.5, Zona Hotelera, Cancun, Mexico: 52-998-883-3333 ext. 138
https://mandalatickets.com/en/cancun/disco/the-city
Cover runs $40-$50 (includes bar) or $25 without. Through the sprawling 3-floor and 8,000 square feet of space this huge club occupies, it's easy to get a drink – they have about 10 bars. Impressive light shows, state-of-the-art sound system, DJs imported from around the world. Though the club doesn't get started till 10:30 at night (runs till about 5 a.m.), the

complex itself opens in the morning, so you can spend the day herein a cabana at the beach, by the pool. Plenty of food and drink all day and night. Different rooms offer different atmospheres. VIP Rooms. Celeb hangout.

COCO BONGO
Blvd. Kukulcan Km 9.5 Plaza Forum, Cancun, Mexico:
+52 998 883 2373/ +52 998 849-4911
www.cocobongo.com/show/cancun/?lang=en
Cover runs $50 during the week and $10 additional on weekends (includes open bar).
Many different kinds of music (salsa, hip-hop, Caribbean, techno and everything else) gets played here in one of the hottest clubs in town. (Holds over 2,500, but you'll still encounter lines). Here at CoCo Bongo, the whole place is a dance floor, from the top of the tables to the top of the bars. Famous around the world for its theme parties.

D'CAVE
Boulevard Kukulcán – KM 9.5, Zona Hotelera, Cancun, Mexico: 52-998-883-3333
https://mandalatickets.com/en/cancun/disco/d-cave
World-famous club frequented by celebrities, socialites, and partyholics. Darkly lit. Live music.

FORUM BY THE SEA

Paseo Kukulcán km. 9.5 zona Hotelera Cancún: 52-998-883-4425

www.forumbythesea.com.mx

WEBSITE DOWN AT PRESSTIME

Oceanfront area has it all. Here you'll find all sorts of nightlife activities: from sports bars to dance clubs, from cheapie taco stands to some of the best dining spots in the area. Lots of shopping as well.

LOBBY LOUNGE
RITZ-CARLTON

Retorno del Rey 36 | Zona Hotelera, Quintana Roo: 52-998-888-0808

www.ritzcarlton.com

For a much more subdued ambience, you'll find a small, intimate club in the Lobby Lounge in the Ritz-Carlton. It opens at 5 for drinks and light snacking, but later, there's a dance floor with a DJ. Not the young, raucous crowds you get in the big clubs.

(They also offer 70 tequilas at the bar and they'll set up tequila flights for you.)

Chapter 5
ATTRACTIONS

TOURS

Everybody in Cancún has got a brother who runs a tour and they can get you a good price. Some of them really are good opportunities and others are rip-offs. We suggest you don't take any of these offers at first. Look around for a bit to get a sense of what is out there and how much it *ought* to cost. Prices fluctuate depending on the season and what conventions might be in town, so ask around. And remember, everybody is your friend when you've got money to spend.

WATER SPORTS

XEL-HA

Carretera Chetumal-Cancun km 240, Quintana Roo:
52-998-883-3143
www.xelha.com

A few miles south of Cancún is Xel-ha, which has transformed itself into a fantasy land of excitement and discovery for those who love the water and all things that live in it.

Here, you can swim with the dolphins for about $100 to $150, depending on how long you want to be in the water with them.

There are dozens of activities such as snorkeling, cliff jumping, tubing, scuba and snuba diving.

('Snuba' diving is for people who aren't certified to scuba dive. You wear a mask attached to tubes that rise to an oxygen tank floating on the surface. The tubes run around 20 feet. Quite liberating.)

They even have a devise called "Sea Trek," a large plastic piece of head gear you put on that covers your whole upper body and rests on your shoulders. You have great underwater views with this device.

The grounds are huge and feature many kinds of environments such as nature trails, cenotes, a giant lagoon, and underwater caves.

EL REY

If you are in Cancún and haven't the time or inclination to commit to a day trip to the further, more well-known sites, but still want to see Mayan ruins, then El Rey is the place for you. You don't even have to leave the city. El Rey is located at kilometer 17 in the south Hotel Zone. The bus goes right by it, and any taxi driver will know where it is.

SEA TURTLES

One of the most memorable events you can experience in Cancún is the turtle season. Cancún is home to two of the world's seven species of sea turtle – the Loggerhead and the Green Turtle. The hospitality industry on the beach is an instrumental player in the conservancy and protection of these endangered species. The laying season begins in April. Incubation lasts about two months, and the last eggs of the season hatch in October. During this season the hotels keep bright lights off the beach at night so as not to disturb the turtles, and many hotels have staff dedicated to sea turtle protection. It is very common to see turtles coming ashore to lay their eggs late at night. This is reported to the local conservancy and the eggs are quickly moved to a protected area where they can incubate in peace. When the baby turtles hatch, guests of the hotels are invited to witness the event and aid in their return to the ocean. Children and adults alike are moved by this magical experience and go home with a new insight into the need to protect the environment and all species of life on Earth.

WHALE SHARKS

The Summer months of June through September are Whale Shark season. During this time the warm waters of the Gulf of Mexico and the Caribbean Sea meet, causing an upswelling of plankton-rich water, which is a feast to these gentle giants. Whale Sharks are the largest fish in the Earth's oceans, sometimes growing to over 40 feet long and weighing over 20

tons. But don't worry, these magnificent creatures
are not a threat to humans, quite the opposite,
actually. During the summer months, Whale Shark
tours leave Cancún daily, filled with happy tourists
excited by the chance to actually swim among these
giant fish.

SWIMMING WITH DOLPHINS

There are a number of dolphinariums located in
Cancún, including some of the major hotels. We ask
that you consider, however, avoiding these
attractions. Dolphins are a highly social and
intelligent creatures. They are taken from their life in
the wide ocean and forced to live out an isolated
existence restricted to a small, often artificial, area for
the amusement of throngs of tourists. We prefer to
leave our cetacean friends free in the wild.

CENOTES

One interesting fact about the Yucatán Peninsula is
that there are no rivers. For various geological and
tectonic reasons, all water flows underground. The

limestone rock covering reservoirs of water in many places has collapsed, leaving open-air sinkholes called Cenotes. These cenotes are often hundreds of feet deep, with crystal-clear cool water. Swimming in these cenotes is an interesting and exciting alternative to a day at the beach. We highly recommend you take at least one day to experience this uniquely Yucatecan pastime.

RUINS

It would be a shame to visit the Yucatán and not see Mayan Ruins. There are hundreds of known Mayan ruins. We list here the ones most convenient to visitors to Cancún. Take bug spray and plenty of water. And you might want to take some bananas to feed the ubiquitous iguanas.

TULUM

You've probably seen the stunning iconic pictures of a Mayan pyramid rising on a cliff above a sandy beach and turquoise waters. That's Tulum, the only significant site that was built on the ocean. Spanish sailors in the early 16th century recorded sailing by and seeing a thriving, colorful Mayan city where we now find grey ruins. The views and ambiance is stunning – our favorite, really. Tulum is located an hour and a half south of Cancún, and there are daily tours from most of the cities in the Yucatán. The site itself is not very large – one can take in the whole place in about an hour – but it is the most photogenic. We recommend arriving early in the day or later in the afternoon, for it can get quite crowded at times. From the parking center one can take the tram for a small fee or walk the quarter mile to the site entrance. There is access to the beaches, so feel free to make a whole day of exploring the ruins then playing in the surf. The souvenir shopping center that has grown up at the parking lot is rather an eye-sore, and the prices are not good, despite what your guide will tell you.

COBA

Coba is about an hour and a half southwest of Cancún. Despite the distance, there are some good reasons to go see this site. Coba is the least restored of all the popular sites, and this gives it a wonderful Indiana Jones feel. There are many buildings that are still covered by jungle. The main pyramid is one of the largest, and visitors can still climb it and look out across the Yucatán jungle. The grounds are quite extensive, so we recommend renting bicycles at the entrance, which adds another enjoyable dimension to your excursion. Watching the crocodiles being fed in the lakes is always a thrill. There are many quaint shops along the road to Coba selling interesting tchotchkes at reasonable prices.

CHICHEN ITZA

Chichen Itza is the most popular Mayan site on the
Yucatán peninsula. The site is listed as one of the
Seven New Wonders of the World. It is a good
distance from Cancún, but dozens of tour buses a day
make the 2 ½ hour trek. We recommend having a
guide for this site. Being the most famous and
developed site, it is also the most restrictive. Visitors
are not allowed in the buildings or to climb the
pyramids. The guides provide a rich narrative to
spark one's imagination and form a bond with the
site. Excellent bilingual guides can be hired for a
reasonable price at the entrance. Many visitors
appreciate the mathematical accuracy and astrological
alignment of the buildings. If possible, we
recommend visiting on either the Spring or Fall
Equinox, where you can join the thousands of people
who come to watch the Descent of the Serpent, a
shadow cast at just the right angle to create the
appearance of a snake descending the Temple of
Kukulcan. After a sweaty day of wandering around

Chichen Itza, we recommend you cool off with a refreshing dip in Ik Kil cenote, a few kilometers away.

ECO ADVENTURE PARKS
Recent years has seen a sharp rise in public interest in ecotourism; and the Yucatán Peninsula, with so much to offer the out-doors-minded traveler, has seen a boom in Eco Adventure Parks. Located within an hour or so of the city, these parks offer a wide range of exciting amusements from zip lines to horse riding to floating along underground rivers. Transportation is best arranged through the parks, as directions can often be vague. We recommend checking with your hotel for tickets, as they often have them at much better prices than you will find at the gate. Here are a few of our favorites.

AKTUNCHEN NATURAL PARK
Located about an hour south of Cancún, Aktun Chen offers an exciting mix of activities for all ages. The caves at this site are magical and we recommend the

tour. If above ground is your thing, go way above ground on their zip line and suspended bridges tour, which travels through the jungle canopy for over a kilometer. They also have a six-acre wildlife zoo with an emphasis on conservation. And don't miss the chance to go swimming and snorkeling in their crystal-clear cenotes.

HIDDEN WORLDS CENOTE PARK

Hidden Worlds has taken tree-top adventure to a whole new level. Besides the regular zip lines, they also have a sky cycle which visitors pedal on lines through the trees. They're big attraction, however, is a new roller coaster style zip line. Scuba diving is offered in the cenotes and there is also a zip line that drops into a cenote. Cave rappelling is an interesting adventure, and when you're tuckered out with all the physical exertion, take a relaxing ride in a jungle buggy. This attraction is about an hour and a half south of the city.

RIO SECRETO

This is one of our favorites. Located in Playa del Carmen, about an hour south of Cancún, Rio Secreto is a stunning series of caves and cenotes which will leave you speechless. There are caverns filled with so many thousands of stalactites and stalagmites that you will think you are in some surreal alien cathedral. This is a tour not to be missed.

SELVATICA

This award-winning eco theme park is closer to
Cancún than most of the others, about half an hour
south. There is a wide array of zip lines, cenotes to
swim in, and lots of different kinds of vehicles to
bump around the jungle trails on.

XAMAN HA AVIARY

The Xaman Ha Aviary is the place to go to see the
wonderful variety of bird species that populate the
Yucatán Peninsula. Here you can see Snowy Egrets,
Pink Flamingoes, Scarlet Macaws and Toucans,
among many, many others. Located in Playa del
Carmen, the aviary is much better priced that many of
the other attractions in the area, and photographers
are welcome to bring their equipment at no additional
charge.

XCARET

Xcaret is one of the largest and oldest eco parks in the
Mayan Riviera. The park features archeological sites,
underground rivers, beaches, lagoons and pools, as

well as educational and interactive exhibits such as aquariums and greenhouses. There are many local species of animal to interact with. In the evening shows featuring the native Mayan legends and customs bring to life the rich and vibrant history of the area.

SIAN KA'AN BIOSPHERE

The Sian Ka'an Biosphere is a leader in ecological conservation and education. Located near Tulum, the center is a model of green technology and sustainable development. A UNESCO World Heritage Site, Sian Ka'an's million acres is home to many species of rare flora and fauna and over twenty archeological sites. Those who love nature and the peace and serenity it offers will find it to their heart's content. We highly recommend renting a kayak.

crafts

Chapter 6
SHOPPING & SERVICES

SHOPPING IN CANCÚN

If you haven't already spent all your money on cenote tours and all-inclusive resorts, there is lots of shopping in Cancún as well. The Hotel Zone has several large and modern malls featuring both Mexican handicrafts and international brands. There are also the requisite chain restaurants and cinemas just as in the US. We suggest you also make the effort to get out of the Hotel Zone and go into downtown Cancún, where you can find the famous Mercado 28, as well as all the chains you know and love in the US.

PLAZA LA ISLA

Blvd. Kukulcán km 12.5, Z.H., 52-998-883-5025
https://islacancun.mx/
This is one of the newest and trendiest of the
shopping centers in the hotel zone. On the Nichupte
Lagoon, the center is built on a series of canals, with
bridges connecting parts of the center, all reminiscent
of Venice. There are many shops of different types,
most of them pricey. Our favorite place to wander
here is the souvenir emporium, where one can find
some good deals. Plaza la Isla also features
restaurants, a disco, and cinema.

PLAZA CARACOL

Blvd Kukulcan Km 8.5, Z.H. 2-998-883-4760
www.plazacaracol.mx/
Plaza Caracol is the biggest mall in Cancún. It is also
very modern. It is centrally located on the Hotel
Zone just north of the Convention Center. There are
many boutiques, including favorites such as Benetton,
Gucci and Ralph Lauren. There are also some very
interesting art galleries. Prices at Plaza Caracol are
pretty good – certainly better that what you'd pay in
the US.

PLAZA LAS AMERICAS

Av. Tulum 260, Downtown, Cancún, 52-998-887-
3863
Located downtown, Cancún's version of a home-
town mall has everything to make you feel at home.
There are a nice assortment of local boutiques,
arcades and fast-food outlets. It also features a JC
Penney and a Sears.

MERCADO 28

Xel-ha Mz. 13 SM 28, 77501 Cancún, Quintana Roo, Mexico: 52-998-892-4303
https://market28cancun.negocio.site/
Mercado Veintiocho. This is Cancún's most popular place to shop for souvenirs. You will enjoy wandering through the many stalls filled with bargains. Here you will find the same items offered in the Hotel Zone, but at much better prices. Haggling for a bargain is part of the fun here, so don't settle for the first price given.

INDEX

100% NATURAL, 30
AIRPORT, 6
AKTUNCHEN NATURAL PARK, 60
ALL RITMO RESORT & WATERPARK, 17
AVALON BACCARA, 17
BACOLI TRATORIA, 35
Blanc Spa, 19
BUS SERVICE, 7
CALYPSO'S GRILL AND MEXICAN FOOD, 31
CANCUN CONVENTION BUREAU, 8
CANCUN MUNICIPAL TOURISM OFFICE, 8
CENOTES, 56
CHIC CABARET & RESTAURANT COSTA MUJERES, 38
CHICHEN ITZA, 59
CITY, THE, 47
COBA, 58
COCO BONGO, 48
ECO ADVENTURE PARKS, 60
EL REY, 54
EL REY DEL CARIBE, 15
ELEFANTA INDIAN CUISINE, 35
EXCELLENCE RIVIERA, 22
FIESTA AMERICANA GRAND CORAL BEACH RESORT & SPA, 22
FORUM BY THE SEA, 49
FRED'S HOUSE & SEAFOOD, 36
GRAND OASIS PALM, 43
GRAND ROYAL LAGOON, 14
HARRY'S PRIME STEAKHOUSE AND RAW BAR, 39
HIDDEN WORLDS CENOTE PARK, 61
HOTEL DEL SOL, 14
HOTEL NYX, 42
HOTEL NYX CANCUN, 42
L'ESCARGOT, 39
LA PALAPA BELGA, 40
LA TRANQUITA GRILL AND BAR, 34
LE BLANC SPA, 18
LIVE AQUA ALL-INCLUSIVE, 25
LOBBY LOUNGE, 49
LOCANDA PAOLO, 36
MAKI TACO, 37

MARRIOTT CASAMAGNA CANCÚN RESORT, 19
MERCADO 28, 67
MOON PALACE GOLF & SPA RESORT, 26
NIZUC RESORT & SPA, 19
OMNI CANCÚN HOTEL, 20
PLAZA CARACOL, 66
PLAZA LA ISLA, 66
PLAZA LAS AMERICAS, 66
Ramona, 20
RENTING A CAR, 7
RESTAURANTE CAREYES, 41
RESTAURANTE CHIANTI, 42
RESTAURANTE LE NATURA, 32
RIO SECRETO, 61
RITZ-CARLTON, 23, 49
RIU PALACE LAS AMERICAS, 24
ROYAL CANCÚN, 27
RUINS, 57
SASI, 43
SAVIO'S BISTRO BY LA DOLCE, 38
SEA TURTLES, 55
SELVATICA, 62

SHOPPING IN CANCÚN, 65
SIAN KA'AN BIOSPHERE, 63
SOTAVENTO HOTEL AND YACHT CLUB, 16
SUITES GABY HOTEL, 16
SUN PALACE, 26
SURFIN BURRITO, 33
SWIMMING WITH DOLPHINS, 56
TAXIS, 6
TEMPTATION RESORT SPA CANCÚN, 21
Terra Nostra, 20
TERRACARIBE HOTEL, 15
Timeshares, 11
TORA MEXICO, 43
Transportation, 6
TULUM, 57
WESTIN LAGUNAMAR CANCÚN, 21
WHALE SHARKS, 55
WHITE BOX, 43
XAMAN HA AVIARY, 62
XBALAMQUÉ, 13
XCARET, 62
XEL-HA, 54